MODERN LIFE

MODERN LIFE

POEMS BY

MATTHEA HARVEY

Graywolf Press
SAINT PAUL, MINNESOTA

Publication of this volume is made possible in part by a grant provided by the Minnesota State Arts Board, through an appropriation by the Minnesota State Legislature; a grant from the Wells Fargo Foundation Minnesota; and a grant from the National Endowment for the Arts, which believes that a great nation deserves great art. Significant support has also been provided by the Bush Foundation; Target; the McKnight Foundation; and other generous contributions from foundations, corporations, and individuals. To these organizations and individuals we offer our heartfelt thanks.

NATIONAL
ENDOWMENT
FOR THE ARTS

MINNESOTA
STATE ARTS BOARD

TARGET.

Published by Graywolf Press
2402 University Avenue, Suite 203
Saint Paul, Minnesota 55114
All rights reserved.

www.graywolfpress.org

Published in the United States of America

ISBN 978-1-55597-480-0
2 4 6 8 9 7 5 3

Library of Congress Control Number: 2007924767

Acknowledgments:
Many, many thanks to the editors of the following journals for giving a home to my poems: *Alaska Quarterly Review, American Poet, Atlanta Review, BOMB, The Canary, Columbia, Copper Nickel, Cue, Forklift, Hayden's Ferry Review, Lumina, Lyric, New Orleans Review, The New Review, Octopus, Perihelion, Pindeldyboz, A Public Space, Southeast Review, Subtropics, Swerve, Tarpaulin Sky, Tempo, Tin House, Volt,* and *Watershed.* The Robo-Boy poems originally appeared in a chapbook, *No One Will See Themself in You,* with drawings by Doug McNamara, published by Delirium Press in 2005.

Cover design: Jeenee Lee Design

Cover art: Matthea Harvey

CONTENTS

IMPLICATIONS FOR MODERN LIFE

The ham flowers have veins and are rimmed in rind, each petal a little meat sunset. I deny all connection with the ham flowers, the barge floating by loaded with lard, the white flagstones like platelets in the blood-red road. I'll put the calves in coats so the ravens can't gore them, bandage up the cut gate and when the wind rustles its muscles, I'll gather the seeds and burn them. But then I see a horse lying on the side of the road and think *You are sleeping, you are sleeping, I will make you be sleeping.* But if I didn't make the ham flowers, how can I make him get up? I made the ham flowers. Get up, dear animal. Here is your pasture flecked with pink, your oily river, your bleeding barn. Decide what to look at and how. If you lower your lashes, the blood looks like mud. If you stay, I will find you fresh hay.

HOW WE LEARNED TO HOLD HANDS

We halved them because we could. It turned out anything with four legs could wobble along on two, anything with two could hop along on one. Leopards. Horses. Kangaroos. Front, back, it didn't matter. Mostly it was teenagers with their parents' Christmas knives who did the cutting. No one knew where the Keepers came from, but they favored covered wagons with billowing sheets tucked in at the edges, puckering like a healing wound. They tied scarves tightly around their chins—men and women—as if to hold the hemispheres of their own heads together. At first they hid the hybrids from us. Their first, clumsiest attempts were the most marvelous—front ostrich, back deer, wind ruffling through first feathers then fur. And the catgoat, all front, who patrolled the shop windows . . . When the sun hit at a certain angle, the battle would begin—cat wanting to see its cat reflection, goat wanting to see goat.

THE GOLDEN AGE OF FIGUREHEADS

First we sloughed off the sailors—when a storm hit we'd lean into it and watch as they slipped into the water. One by one we washed our decks clean, pried their rough fingers from our rudders. Now we can finally go where we want—swooping around archipelagos in packs, zigzagging along the paths the sun and moon make, skimming the Pacific solo. Sometimes we'll peer into the water to catch a glimpse of our old enemies, the anchors, glinting at the bottom of the ocean, the thick ropes that once tethered us to them twisting and turning in the currents like snakes charmed out of their baskets by the song of the sea. We don't mind that our masts are crusted with salt, our rigging grows ragged, our bright paint—reds and golds and greens— has faded so that we're pencil sketches of what we once were. We don't even mind the barnacles that muffle our mouths: after all, we have no common language. The ship with a bird's head wants to squawk with the gulls that forage from its sails, would follow them into the water when they dive for fish if only it could. Her ladyship, who trails sheets of seaweed like floaty green skirts, is lovesick for the sailor who used to stain her lips with wine before each voyage. But there is always the rain. When it falls hard enough we can't tell which way is up, which way is down. Then we're like the earth before the equator was invented, like the giant tenor who unbuckles his belt and lets out his one truest note.

IF SCISSORS AREN'T THE ANSWER, WHAT'S A DOLL TO DO?

The dotted lines go everywhere. Up the ceiling and around the chandelier. Down the basement steps and straight into the lint tray. In some places the lines are black, like the ones that reframe each framed ancestral photograph on my Wall of Ancestral Photographs. In others they are silvery; hard to see in bright light. I avoid those rooms. I shuffle around in my paper slippers, tiptoe over the envelopes fanning out from the mailslot. I sit in the second-floor window and watch leashes strain between dogs and people; I keep the volume on the stereo low. Sometimes late at night a car—wild, impervious—guns by, swerving in and out of its lane. The next morning, the pansies are re-dotted with dew.

YOU KNOW THIS TOO

The bird on the gate and the goat nosing the grass below make a funny little fraction, thinks the centaur. He wonders if this thought is more human than horse, more poetry than prose. Sometimes it's hard not to abandon the whole rigmarole of standing at the counter—using a knife and fork to politely eat his steak and peas—to go outside and put his head in the grass. But what his stomach wants, his tongue won't touch; what his mouth wants, his stomach recoils from. Through the restaurant window he sees flashes of silver and pink in the river. It's so clogged with mermaids and mermen, there's no room for fish. And under the bridge, a group of extremist griffins, intent on their graffiti—*Long Live the Berlin*. . . . The spray paint runs out and while they're shaking the next can in their clenched claws, the centaur spells out *Wall* on his napkin, and sketches next to it a girl in sequins getting sawed in half.

THE FUTURE OF TERROR / 1

The generalissimo's glands directed him
to and fro. *Geronimo!* said the über-goon
we called God, and we were off to the races.
Never mind that we could only grow
gray things, that inspecting the horses' gums
in the gymnasium predicted a jagged
road ahead. We were tired of hard news—
it helped to turn down our hearing aids.
We could already all do impeccable imitations
of the idiot, his insistent incisors working on
a steak as he said *there's an intimacy to invasion.*
That much was true. When we got jaded
about joyrides, we could always play games
in the kitchen garden with the prisoners.
Jump the Gun, Fine Kettle of Fish and Kick
the Kidney were our favorites. The laws
the linguists thought up were particularly
lissome, full of magical loopholes that
spit out medals. We had made the big time,
but night still nipped at our heels.
The navigator's needle swung strangely,
oscillating between the oilwells
and *ask again later.* We tried to pull ourselves
together by practicing quarterback sneaks
along the pylons, but the race to the ravine
was starting to feel as real as the R.I.P.'s
and roses carved into rock. Suddenly the sight
of a schoolbag could send us scrambling.

THE FUTURE OF TERROR / 2

The gift certificates advertised
goggle-eyed paratroopers attempting a fall
from grace, but the heart-lung machines
strapped to their packs kept them loving
and breathing long beyond when they were supposed
to live. Happy-go-lucky is just a decision to proceed
with an assumption of happiness and luck.
The Observation Station gained a toehold,
appeared on houseflags, had us hooked.
Don't get the impression we weren't
all dialing information every hour: we were,
if only intracranially. In an inversion of
the usual itinerary, we felt a jolt of bullets
before we even entered the jungle. Juxtapose that
with the killing frost which knotted the vines
and made the whitefish shiver underwater
and one can account for our general sense of
get it out, leave it alone, leave it.
We would have written that on our license plates
if not for the bureaucratic line of scrimmage
we knew in our livers we'd never cross.
A mailing machine can't sort for meaning or memory
but it gets the merchandise to your door. It gets you
your mitten money. It's only natural to neglect
the near-point, the one thing you can actually see.
Our poets were Pied Pipers handing out
photocopies—parroting, parenthesizing.
With the right pomade you can smooth over
anything. In the precinct they were making predictions
based on prehistory, listening to old recordings
of preacher-birds. The Reform Bill wanted
us on risers with rosettes pinned to our breasts
while we sang the same song again.

THE FUTURE OF TERROR / 3

We wore gasmasks to cross the gap.
Goodnight, said the gravediggers, goodnight.
We looked heavenward but kept our hands
down when they asked for volunteers
so they simply helped themselves.
Our protestations sounded like herons
on the hi fi. Even armed with invoices,
it's human nature to proceed inch-meal.
We were a sad jumble of journeymen and here's
the kicker: a few of us had never been in love.
Sure, we shared our laminated letters with them,
made models out of lard, but there's no way to leap-frog
that sort of thing. The lieutenant thought the unloved
made better lookouts, though mostly they read
magazines stashed in their mackintoshes
and came back with useless reports on
the micromotions of magpies. When I looked
at the nametape inside my uniform, I missed
my mother. I knew where I was headed:
a spot in the necropolis with plastic nasturtiums.
Periodically, we started projects: one man
made dents in the shape of stars on the inside
of his P.O. Box with a Phillips head screwdriver.
We all carried plump pods filled with poison
that quivered as we made our daily rounds
of the ruins. Giving sadness the run-around
was even harder after our sergeant succumbed
to Salt Lake Syndrome. At night in our
smokeproof sleeping cars, we dreamed of
sharp sticks that would make wounds
a simple surgeon's knot couldn't fix
and other ways to pry the lid off the terrarium.

We got most of our gear from
an abandoned general store—gnat spray
for our sojourns under the gumtrees,
seed for the garden warblers in case
they ever sang again. Out of glass blocks
we built a glorious latrine which we meant
to show the governor when he arrived
with his hand on his heart, but for some reason
we hesitated. Was it the rust on the hinge
of his briefcase? His car horn's half-hearted honk?
We just didn't hit it off this time. Maybe
we were tired of the same old hyphenated
hush-hush. Having no idol made us ill-tempered.
We stole the pilots' inclinometers
so they didn't know if they were going up or down
unless they were naturally level-headed.
We locked Frank in the Isolation Booth.
By the time the jubilee came around
we were all on probation, so we made a mini-parade
out of jumping beans and ants on a plaid rug
in the barracks though that ended
in a knock-down-drag-out fight too.
The Listening Post was right under a linden tree
so all we ever heard was leaves falling but
it wasn't manly to write about that in your report.
When the migratory birds arrived, there was mold
on their beaks and a musty smell coming from
their under-feathers. We mounted the public address
system behind the proscenium where they used to have
puppet shows, then walked round-shouldered
through the rubble. A sandpiper squawked

out a storm warning and got sucked up
into the clouds. We were sweaty and ready
to surrender. What was there left to say?
We turned on the teleprompter.

If there were gamebirds in our gables,
shouldn't we shoot them ourselves?
Thus we went glass-faced into glory.
We had our hearts set on staying here,
so our steps seemed more hesitation
waltz than straight-ahead tango.
We danced the hokey pokey on holy days—
put your left arm in heaven, your right leg in hell
and in the hubbub of shake-it-all-about,
we didn't hear the hoofbeats. The illuminati
spoke to us over the intercom via interpreters.
Meanwhile we had iodine dribbling from
our wounds and itch mites in our blankets.
Ours was not a job to joke about.
In the lantern-light, the lawn speckled
with lead looked lovely. We would live this
down by living it up. My pile of looseleaf
was getting smaller—I wrote in margins,
through marmalade stains, on the backs of maps.
I put a piece of mica in the microwave and before
the explosion it made the mirage I'd imagined.
I was hoping for a noticeable increase in nutmeats
or a one night stand in the oubliette. I outwept
everyone at the pageant, even the children
from the poorhouse playing possum.
We studied the protocol for astronaut removal
the minute we saw his spit hit planet earth
on the spaceship window. But though the scandal
reverberated round-the-clock, we had to let it
slide. He was up there turning somersaults
while we spun ever-so-slowly below.

There were girls waiting at the gate
but we were homonyms away from
understanding each other, like halve
and have, like "let me hold you" and "I hold you
responsible." Hospital bed or house arrest
were the idylls we lived for. I promised to name
my firstborn Influenza for a better shot at the flu.
A knot of spectators got killed and unraveled
into the lake. We discussed the particular
lattice patterns we liked to use in our lasagna,
never mind that the party line was
that we were lucky to get linseed cake.
Oh the milk of magnesia *that* required—
mouthful after mouthful from mirrored spoons.
The die landed on a one-spot, which was exactly
how far we were going to get—one step
into the orchard opposite, then chalk outlines
for everyone. The pep rallies were horrible.
The only thing that helped with the palpitations
was to hold a paper nautilus to your ear and listen
to the sighing of its parallel seas. Somewhere
in there were seagulls whose pinfeathers
were starting to unfurl, families taking Polaroids
of the piles of quahogs they'd collected,
a shopkeeper opening his shutters while
his space heater happily hummed with oil.
In there, the Spite Fence had yet to be invented.

We spun the globe to forget
our grievances. Greenland: gone.
The Gulf, a blurry gouache.
We went on hayrides and watched
the gulls glide overhead, though
our health insurance no longer covered
hayrides, only icewater, aspirin
and iris inspections, which the individualists
outside the gate said infringed on their inalienable
rights. They were just jumpy from
the fake battles—all the actors keeling over
with ketchup dripping from their lips.
The Kiss of Peace, we called it, just to
annoy the know-it-alls. The latest liquor
(a liquid Lucite stronger than any we'd tasted
before) made our losses loom a little less.
And there was the TV melodrama (on at eight)
about the matchmaker we all loved—
we cheered when she nodded, signaling
she'd made a match, never mind that her
offbeat choices were often obviously calamitous.
Had I pictured myself as a patriot on payroll,
planting stories so we'd have one positive
poll per quarter? It was no paradise
fielding the quizzical looks, repeating,
I do not recollect, always sticking to script,
but I knew my shelflife. I knew to hum
"The Star-Spangled Banner" when I palmed
that extra soda. I knew how not to look
like I was dreaming of summer.

THE FUTURE OF TERROR / 8

Stories about the boy raised by gazelles
haunted us. As the Gravity Hinge closed
down the day again, in our gloom
we couldn't help but picture him hoofing
through the hazy air, unaware. Each extra
day was a literal gift of habeas corpus.
We ignored inoculation instructions
and read *Intimations of Immortality*
to the invalids instead. We couldn't curse
the goddamned chiefs of staff
except inwardly, but we could make kites
in case we ever saw the sky again.
We could listen for a knock at the door.
We were on our last legs, 8 in total, four
covered in lesions. I wrote *lotion* on my list
right under *try to live the livelong day.*
If I sniffled, it was because of an excess of mucus,
nothing more. My hands and feet were mauve—
too little motion, too many menthols,
and when I stretched I felt needlefish
like a northerly wind along my spine.
There were murmurs they might open
the door. I was ready to outsprint everyone.
I had a parcel for gazelle boy. He was somewhere
on the peninsula, grazing on a patch of grass
as plump as a pincushion. He'd prick up
his ears, and then quid pro quo, he'd show me
where to find rainwater, which roots to eat.
Nibble, nibble, repeat. We'd roam the rocky coasts,
gallop down slopes with satellites as our stars.
But no surprises please. Please no surprises.
I couldn't stomach it if he ever spoke.

We gathered broken gadgets until our eyes
glazed over. One gizmo said *going going
gone,* then made a silly exploding sound.
I ground it under my boot one night
after too many actual gunshots
zinged through the hacienda's already-
shattered windows. Some haven.
I had a head cold which made it hard
for me to hear the bullets coming—
sometimes I ducked when someone hiccupped.
We'd found two intellectuals hiding in separate
parts of the basement and when we put them
in a room together they instantly started lobbing
outdated ideas back and forth as if this were the time
for badminton. They were informers all right.
Eventually we put them in a kayak and sent them
off down the river without the key word,
which despite their loquaciousness, they'd never
guess. Plus there were magnetic mines
in the river and theirs was a metal boat.
That morning while the minister muttered
about emulating molecules, I could tell
from studying the others' profiles that they too
were wondering what was going on off-screen
in the ocean. Could we really keep on this way,
picking our paths according to pH balances,
proposing quasi-constitutional amendments
about portion-size? The shed in the meadow
had gone to seed. Sometimes I sprawled
there, out of sight of the sentinel.

At the last gathering, we each got a bowl
of gelatin. I watched a grasshopper in the greenhouse
crashing against the glass walls. There were a few civilians
hold-outs in the high rises hoarding their hemlock
way past intermission. By now we were indifferent
to them. Their pale faces at the windows no longer
made us shiver in our thin khaki jackets.
If only we could think of something to joke
about we could literally have had the Last Laugh,
but my stupid mind kept making long-range
plans despite the middle ground between
now and then being riddled with mines.
One of the guys, nickname Milquetoast, started
work on a monument—to what, no one knew.
It was part trash heap, part mosaic. . . . I added
a nebula made from nylons wound around nails
which I imagined would eventually oxidize
into the perfect hazy orange. People came to
observe us, began shouting out suggestions.
To placate one paralyzed soldier who brought us
a pedometer permanently set at zero, we designed
a spine of fake pearls. Other people left us pinking shears,
a pram in pieces, a pumice stone—things that had
once been precious to them. We put everything in.
The army had abandoned its rallies and raffles, even
the games of Raise the Red Flag. Our rifles rusted
on the ground and the sculpture grew. One day
its silicon steeple began to show over the supply shed.
I don't know who took the first shot, but I know
that we all joined in. There was a wild spray of bullets,
along with whatever else we could find to throw.
When it crumbled we stamped on the ruins.
It felt great to tear something down again.

From the gable window, we shot
at what was left: gargoyles and garden gnomes.
I accidentally shot the generator
which would have been hard to gloss over
in a report except we weren't writing reports
anymore. We ate our gruel and watched
the hail crush the hay we'd hoped to harvest.
I found a handkerchief drying on a hook
and without a hint of irony, pocketed it.
Here was my hypothesis: we were inextricably
fucked. We'd killed all the inventors and all
the jesters just when we most needed humor
and invention. The lake breeze was lugubrious
at best, couldn't lift the leaves. As the day lengthened,
we knew we'd reached the lattermost moment.
The airlift wasn't on its way. Make-believe
was all I had left but I couldn't help but see
there was no "we"—you were a mannequin
and I'd been flying solo. I thought about
how birds can turn around mid-air, how
the nudibranch has no notion it might need
a shell. Swell. I ate the last napoleon—
it said *Onward!* on the packaging.
There was one shot left in my rifle.
I polished my plimsolls.
I wrapped myself in a quilt.
So this is how you live in the present.

INSIDE THE GOOD IDEA

From the outside it is singular. One wooden horse. Inside ten men sit cross-legged, knees touching. No noun has been invented yet to describe this. They whisper that it would be like sitting in a wine barrel if the curved walls were painted red. The contents are not content. They would like some wine. They quarrel about who gets to sit in the head until finally the smallest man clambers in, promising to send messages back to the belly. He can only look out of one eye at a time. At first there is nothing to report. Black, Dark, The Occasional Star. Then Quiet Footsteps Mixed with Questions. The children are clamoring for it to be brought inside the walls. The head sends back another message which gets caught in the throat: *They are bringing their toy horses to pay their respects to us, brushing their tiny manes, oiling the little wheels. It must be a welcome change from playing war.*

A THEORY OF GENERATIONS

You're it.
You're it.
You're it.

THE EMPTY PET FACTORY

My love works the night shift at the Empty Pet factory. I've only been there once and I still have nightmares about the heartless hamster he had me hold in my hand, the rooms of inside-out Chihuahuas drying on racks. The pet waitlist keeps getting longer. Celebrities love them. To the outside world you can continue to seem like America's sweetheart, simpering, *I do hope the fox gets away* as you dig your heels into a horse filled to the brim with vitriol and follow the flash of red over the hedge. Only the keenest eye could detect that you just screwed your horse's shiny eyes into its head after emptying handfuls of hate into its big glossy body. This morning, over breakfast, he tells me excitedly that they've perfected the Unrequited Love Puppies—their chubbiness will serve as camouflage for the love bulging and straining against their doubly reinforced seams. He's getting toast crumbs all over his uniform. One lands inside the Empty Pet logo on his lapel—an outline of an indeterminate mammal. The cages stacked in the corners are quiet. The parrots think it's night when the covers are on. They're all factory rejects—couldn't learn to keep quiet the things they've been told. At night, when he's gone, sometimes I turn on all the lights and let them squawk the test secrets they've been fed in the laboratory, a glorious cacophony of *I hate your mother, Your best friend made a pass at me* and *I never liked your nose.* I think one day he'll come home and find me in there with them, repeating over and over again, *You don't understand me. You never have.*

ESTAMOS EN VIVO, NO HAY ALTERNATIVO

Down here in the land of slammed doors,
the factory puffs its own set of clouds

into the sky. Fake larks fly through
them, lifelike. Let's not go into contractions

of can't and won't or how behind the line of trees,
the forest is gone. Dip that tiny brush into

your paintbox and mix up something nice
and muddy for me. We've got a lock

on the moon so now it goes where we want it—
mostly proms, sometimes lobbies.

This is my favorite sign: "Live girls, live action!"
and in smaller but still flashing lights:

"girl on girl, girl on _____." Among the permutations,
there's no "girl on hands and knees begging for her life."

No one we know wants it that badly.

MUSEUM OF THE MIDDLE

You're walking down the middle of the road when you start sinking. Each white stripe gets successively softer, like strips of gum left out in the sun. You pass daffodils, coffins, and fossils until you're at the earth's core. The doorknob burns your hand but inside is the usual cool, museum-ish hush. A tapestry (2' x 48') charting the rise and fall of the middle class is backlit so that the stitched line fluoresces like a heartbeat on a monitor. Most prized is a worm segment in the foyer, a pink accordion mounted on black velvet and framed in gold. They say a worm can live if you cut it in half but not if you extract its exact middle. In the next room and spilling into the one after that is the ever-expanding gallery of middle management—almost all white men. Today there are two special exhibits—to your left, Hermes and Other Intermediaries; to your right, The Middle Distance: Forgotten Focus. In each painting, the foreground and background have been blacked out, leaving fragments of fields, flagstones, the occasional midsized sheep. But why are *you* here? Do your parents love you exactly 5% less than your brother and 5% more than the dog? What museum-worthy mediocrity do the curators see in you?

THE LOST MARCHING BAND

is often seen snaking over hilltops, the cymbal player holding his cymbals aloft like the golden ears of a giant mouse. Only the mouse shows up in bedtime stories. Parents never mention the deer found bludgeoned by flutes, imprints of keys on their cheeks and haunches. As children themselves, they'd been rushed past the oboe player found abandoned in the street, still keeping a reed moist in her mouth though one sleep in the sun had baked all music out of it. Sometimes, after a long rain has filled the tuba and the baritone and the band has taken turns drinking, they revert to their old ways. They find a field and start spelling out words—GO TEAM, or SPIRIT. Pivot, turn, pivot. It comforts them to do it. Their unsnapped spats flap in the wind. The twirler's baton is a twig. The conductor's last gold button fell into a puddle years ago where it shone over a scene long forgotten: two teams, a ball, a game.

WORD PARK

Proper nouns are legible in any light and like to stay near their cages. They're the saunterers and the preeners, the peacocks who walk up to you and unfurl their fan of feathers hello. To see a shy one, position yourself between two trees; eventually it'll get whisked into a sentence and will have to come out from the shadows. We stock the park with packs of verbs and ands, so the odds are in your favor. Lessons in tracking are given every hour on the hour. You'll learn to go unnoticed behind a lamppost so you can get a glimpse of a squabble—COAT's flapping shadow tussling with WEARING because it wants to be the verb. The comma is the timid creature (ankle-height, cringing) you'll spot when you pause to look at the map, the dash is the sprinter in a thin coat of rain. Take a left for indirect object, for conjunctions, straight ahead. Officially, the exotics are extinct, but you've heard about watchers in the cities training their binoculars on ledges half-hidden by air conditioners, scanning the gutters for pairs of bright eyes. They know the ruses unsanctioned words use. They roll in the dirt to hide their vivid feathers. According to the tabloids, CHOCOLATED made it half way across the country, hopping from schoolyard to schoolyard in a convincing coat of mud, and last week VERYING was spotted hiding in the wake of a ferry. One watcher got a picture before the authorities harpooned it. In the photograph the water is bluer than blue.

[   ]

A child glanced up at her father and they named that "Buttercup." The stripes on the road (not the new ones but the ones the wheels had worn away) they named "Ghost Morse Code." They named the difference between a photograph of a red barn and a photo-realist painting of the same red barn, "One-Minute-Past-the-Hour." They left no stone unturned, naming the rock's light gray belly, the smears of soil that stuck to it, the indentation left behind in the ground. Even the damp smell of centipedes warranted a word. The Naming Books were stored in warehouses across the country at exactly 64 degrees. There wasn't much that wasn't in them, a nation of Adams flinging names across the land had seen to that. Some people rebelled and there was a name for that too. Somewhere there was one hotel with no name, no sign and no list of guests. If you managed to find it, you might come upon a crowd huddled around a group of waiters who were flinging water at vents expelling such icy-cold air that the water would freeze in a random and unclassifiable manner, then melt as quickly as it had frozen. Or a row of long tables with bowls of something that was neither sauce nor soup and outside the window, a bonfire of pink letter paper.

SET YOUR SIGHTS

"Let your fur hood soften
the periphery," says the psychiatrist.

When that doesn't work,
he gives me the snowgoggles. Split

second, split minute—he's taken
my ogle, the angle I was working:

180° of the igloo and the snowshoe strut.
Listening quiets the glistening,

slits line things up.
So this is focus. Fine.

Fine.

SATELLITE STORAGE INC.

The satellites look like rusty metal cubes—some minimalist's project gone bad or boring. With all their flying parts folded into themselves, it's as if they've gone back in time. They're baby birds with gummed eyelids, knowing nothing beyond the nest's perimeter. The soldier in charge pays the phone bill each month but no one calls. He keeps the satellites at the ready, is sure that if he flipped the switches on their underbellies, they would whir and start up as if they had just been shut down. He has various strategies to remind them of flight. When a tree hits a power line, announcing *storm!*, he hops off whatever barstool he's sitting on and drives to the facility, opens all the windows and doors and lets the wind and rain rip through. For a few years, he kept a canary there. He has filmstrips of sunsets and recordings of space, one yellow spotlight, one white, and a tiny model of Phoenix, AZ, which he places underneath the satellites one by one, in rotation. When he sees the sad girl standing in the corner at a party, he knows exactly what to do.

YOU NEVER SEEMED SO HUMAN

So we married in the UFO:
they didn't know what we meant
when you said *pony* and
I whispered *mountain*
in the chilly Hall of Collectibles.

WAC-A-MOLE REALISM™

At the carnival, Robo-Boy sees only things he recognizes. The Ferris Wheel is an overgrown version of his own bells and whistle eyes. His Flashers, his mother calls them. The Tilt-A-Whirl is the angle his head tilts when the Flirt Program goes into effect, usually in the vicinity of a Cindy or a Carrie, though once he found himself tilting at the school librarian which caused him to wheel in reverse into the Civil War section knocking over a cart of books that were waiting to be shelved under B. There's a dangerously low stratosphere of pink cotton-candy clouds being carried around by the children. If Robo-Boy goes near them, the alarms will go off. It's the kind of sticky that would cause joint-lock for sure. In a darker, safer corner Robo-Boy finds the Whack-A-Mole game. He pays a dollar and starts whacking the plastic moles on their heads each time they pop up from the much-dented log. He wins bear after bear. It's only when he's lugging them home, the largest one skidding face-down along the sidewalk getting dirt on its white nose and light blue belly, that he remembers the program: Wac-A-Mole Realism™—the disc on the installer's desk. Suddenly it all fits together: the way a deliciously strange thought will start wafting out of his unconscious—and then WHAM, it disappears.

EMPHASIS ON MISTER OR PEANUT, ROBO OR BOY

In the chapters on Special Children, the parenting books stress the need for role models. Hence the silver-framed portraits of Mr. Peanut, the Michelin Man and Mrs. Butterworth in silver frames on Robo-Boy's bureau. Robo-Boy has never quite known what to do with them. For a while he thought they might be estranged relatives, especially since his parents never mentioned them. Mr. Peanut, debonair as Fred Astaire, looks like the kind of uncle who might tell you over steak and a cigar that with a pair of gloves and a monocle slotted over your eyesocket, you can have your pick of the ladies. Mrs. Butterworth figured more in Robo-Boy's brief religious phase—there's something holy in her maple syrup glow, and in her shape, something of the Buddha. The Michelin Man is the one who worries him. With his perpetual thumbs-up and cheerful expression he looks like he might be hoping to hitchhike his way the hell out of here—

NO ONE WILL SEE THEMSELF IN YOU

In the sketches, the eyes looked just right: luminous green with lids set on "random" to blink. But now with the robot right there on the table taking its first test breaths under his fingertips (still silver, still an "it," with skin and gender slated for tomorrow), the inventor can see his mistake. He's given it miniature traffic light eyes, always green for go. As a child he used to watch one from his bedroom window, swinging on a wire like charm on a bracelet, its housing painted standard government mustard. It was his Magic 8 ball, his Tarot pack, his fill-in-the-blank: if he opened his eyes on green it meant go downstairs, pretend you had a nightmare (the details—type of monster, setting of chase-scene—are negligible as long as you say your parents saved you—*together*—in the end). Yellow meant wake your sister. Red almost always meant a nasty scraping sound as the tailpipe hit the one tilted slab in the driveway. The inventor closes his eyes, opens them again. Why hadn't he given the robot pupils, that nervous aperture that shape-shifts from circle to surfboard with the flick of a light switch. His ex-lover used to say to him, "lend me your mini-mirrors." He doesn't believe in any of that inkwell-of-the-soul crap, but still he fiddles with the wiring behind each eye, unscrews a circle of green lights in the center and the robot does look better, more human. But on the computer screen he sees what the robot sees: a blind spot right in the center of his vision, a dartboard with a black bull's-eye, a hole that swallows anything he turns to see—

MINOTAUR, NO MAZE

At the DMV Robo-Boy presents his hands. It makes you wonder. Why would they bother to engrave on each palm a life line (deep and long), a head line (joined to his life line meaning he has "a cautious, sometimes fearful nature") and a heart line (faint and dotted, that figures) and forget to give him fingerprints? The woman looks down at the form. She has little epaulettes of dandruff on each shoulder. "Is there a reason the subject cannot be fingerprinted? An amputation? Current injury? Other, please explain." She looks up and then back down again. And so Robo-Boy falls under the category of "other" again. Nervously, he picks at his wrist with his fingernail (fingernails he has) until a bit of beige flakes off and he can see his silver undercoat glinting through. His mother keeps a little can of Skinspray #439 for touch-ups in her bedside table drawer along with her pearls and her vitamins. Once she broke a bottle of foundation in her bag and when he looked inside it seemed lined with her skin. It pleased and scared him—he half expected a pair of eyes to blink open above the zipper-mouth of the inside pocket. Instant baby sister. The woman is signaling for her supervisor—first subtly with her eyebrows, but soon she's making huge loops and whorls with her arms. Robo-Boy looks at her desk, her phone, her black coffee mug—there are fingerprints everywhere, little gray mazes that all lead back to her big gold nametag, which reads HOW MAY I HELP? I'M (and then scrawled in smeared ink) Janice.

ROBO-BABY

When Robo-Boy feels babyish, he has the option of really revert-
ing. The button is tiny and awkwardly placed beneath his left shoul-
der blade, but he can just reach it with a chopstick. One well-placed
poke and he's folding in like an accordion until he's a simple 2'x2'x2'
cube: Robo-Baby. Cute. Compact. One year, scouring the house for
hidden Christmas presents, he found the box he came in tucked in
the back of the closet under the stairs. The bad font on the outside
(of course they used *Futura*) embarrasses him, but he has to admit
he kind of likes the inside of the box. It's covered with cartoon pan-
els of scenes from his supposed past. He recognizes the scenes as
memories, but he likes looking at the flat version without the im-
ported sense data attachments. Like most parents who adopt robots,
his fast-forwarded through his first three years. On Day One he puts
everything in his mouth, pulls himself up by holding onto the coffee
table and takes his first steps. On Day Two he says no to everything,
begins and perfects potty training and throws three twenty-minute
tantrums. On day three, he invents an imaginary friend and develops
a fear of peacocks. He has a year's-worth of blurry baby memories
for each of these days, but he can tell where the switch from pre-
recorded to actual memories happens. In the pre-memories his par-
ents' faces are cut-outs from their wedding photograph pasted onto
bodies that don't quite match. In his first real memory (a whispered,
"Honey, should we know how to turn him off, just in case?") their
faces ripple like ponds disturbed by giant fish fighting beneath the
surface before they settle into twin grins.

LONESOME LODESTONE

Robo-Boy is in band practice when it happens. A piccolo hits him squarely in the chest, then stays there, as if super-glued. He looks up and sees a metal wall consisting of the brass section (one tuba, two baritones, four trumpets, one French horn) lurching towards him—thank god for Thinkfast™ and Reflex™, which have saved him from countless blacktop humiliations. The wall of gold metal hits the door with a giant clang as it closes behind him, then slowly slides to the floor, the treasure hoard of some mad musician king. Robo-Boy runs home, noticing the stop signs bending towards him, the rings in the jewelry store pressing their sparkling noses to the glass, the grinning bracelets. The quilting circle doesn't see him through the window, but their needles take note, rising in his direction like plants that seek out the sun. One needle straining towards this new center of the universe pricks Mrs. Eisenstein's finger. Consider the drop of blood that falls onto the flowered fabric the official marker of the beginning of Robo-Boy's puberty. At home, locked in his room, Robo-Boy is spitting out paperclips, covering his ears so he won't hear the sound of the pots and pans rattling downstairs in the kitchen.

MOVING DAY

When it comes to spatial puzzles, Robo-Boy is a natural. Before putting the toaster in a cardboard box he slides a slim paperback into each of its two slots. (This will later result in one toasted *A Farewell to Arms* and a pile of ash that was once *The Volcano Lover*. His mom will look at the chrome box in flames and wonder if he is trying to tell her something.) He crams two pillowy bags of flour into the blender where they wrinkle like elephant ankles. (Later again, when his mom opens the lid, a puff of flour will escape like a weak protest—*no!*) When she hands him the box of packing sheets to put between the Sunday plates, she doesn't know she's giving him something he's been looking for. He learned the word last week in English class: subjectivity—*proceeding from or taking place in a person's mind rather than the external world.* He got it right on the quiz but only understood it after his friend (his only friend) Lucy explained it to him: *You know how if you're in a bad mood a wet dog looks one way and if you're in a good mood it looks another? It's like wearing tinted glasses, only on the inside.* Robo-Boy doesn't know but he wants to. Describe it, he says, over and over again. Robo-Boy has five emotions, HAPPY, SAD, ANGRY, CONFUSED, and CONTENT. When he switches from one to another his body makes the same sound his dad's Acura makes when shifting from first into second gear, second into third. He's learned to clear his throat to mask the grinding sound. Robo-Boy holds the thin sheet of Styrofoam to the light and thinks, "subjectivity." Mind whirring, he wraps the plates in newspaper and stows the sheets in his suitcase. The next night, in the new house, he starts the project, labeling them as he goes. For MELANCHOLY TINGED WITH SWEETNESS he soaks the sheet in gloppy gray paint, pastes on ripped photographs of factories and sprays the mess with Chanel No. 5. For TEARS TURNING TO LAUGHTER he sprinkles the top half of the sheet with glitter and paints a baseline of blue. Tomorrow he will go on a walk with the sheets stowed in his backpack. He'll sit on a fence and look at the clouds, through exhilaration, hysteria, delight, despair.

OTHER (BE SPECIFIC)

The driftwood fencepost
is doubly downed, comma after soil,

comma after sea. Rain falls
around the horse-space.

Yes, I think I'll have my say-so.
I invented that glint in your eye

with my version of terrarium,
this thin glass coat.

I know what you'll say and it's true.
We may already be drowning

if we choose to take the aerial view.

RESTRICTED VISTA

Where they've punched holes in the roof,
twenty tubes of sunlight slide through.

Rattatatat. The paparazzi clatter
up the ladder and now their eyes

are shooting sight-lines past you,
through you. They're in the "about" section

watching the dreams below. You're here
because you've seen things, because you see things:

red ground behind your eyelids,
panoramas pulsing beneath each shoe.

YOUR OWN PERSONAL SUNSHINE

One day it slipped under my umbrella—a basketball-sized yolk that nudged the handle out of my hand and when I squinted up at it, I had to admit the rain had stopped falling. Puddles receded, nay recoiled from my once-wet feet and around me suddenly everything was a-something, achirp, aflutter. I was afraid. Where was my taxidermist version of the world—trees gnarled with scruples, antlers of impossible choices mounted on the wall? Pollen-specks of sunshine were impinging on my white catastrophe dress. That's when I did it. I pushed that yellow provocateur—never mind my sizzling palms— through the door of a lighting store. Let *it* feel like everyone else.

FREE ELECTRICITY

First the prong marks appeared on my cheeks as if someone had scratched equals signs under my eyes. Three days later there was an aching just behind my knee and I found the first socket. I studied it with a hand mirror. It was exactly the shape of the outlet next to my bed—two rectangular openings and below them a hole like the mouth of a tunnel. I can remember the order in which they appeared—one on the side of my neck, another on my shoulderblade, another in the sole of my foot, yet another at my wrist—but I don't remember who first used me. I remember folding up my miniskirts and short-sleeved shirts and wearing clothes that covered every inch, so perhaps it was a lover who discovered my hidden talent—took the alarm clock and plugged it into my foot—or my sister who positioned me close to the blender when the power went out. At first it was just as a favor. "Would you mind. . . ." "Would it be too much trouble. . . ." Etc. But soon they didn't ask. It's all so long ago now—I've grown used to my cocoon of orange cords. Someone kind left a gap at my eyes, so at night I can see the red switches of the piles of powerstrips blinking and imagine the city running on whatever strange surge (not quite sugar, not quite caffeine) flows through my veins. That's me in the hum of your fan, me in the crackle of your TV, me lighting up every last lightbulb.

OUT OF ORDER

Today it's about truth and hope
and there are no ha-ha's
between me and the living.
World, I'm no one
to complain about you.

ONCE AROUND THE PARK WITH OMNISCIENCE

The man with the metal detector hovering over the elm's elephantine roots has no idea he just missed a buried paint can (color: beige ballet) containing six letters and an engagement ring. Pug owners are 90% more likely to deny that they look like their pets than other dog owners. The girl in the woolen hat holding her camera out to capture herself and her pug on the bench is in the 10% minority and cherishes her own buggy brown eyes. Mittens on strings are only metaphorical to people without children. A jogger sees a small child with red mittens dangling from her sleeves and thinks *memory*, then imagines running around the park next Sunday with a big pair of silver scissors, tiny mittens blossoming from the mud puddles in her wake. *Mothers Beware the Mitten Marauder!* reads the headline in the *Post*. Truly it's exhausting how many minds there are to swoop in and out of. Thoughts criss-cross the paths like branches; kites get caught in them. Birds collide with dreams and are found dead on the road. Sometimes a storm is the only answer. I stir up such a wind it blows them all out of the park. Then I pour down so much rain that the park sparkles with puddles, a thousand YOU ARE HERE signs blinking up at me and only me, until some intrepid soul comes stomping through with his loud thoughts of dinner.

DINNA' PIG

Members of the Family rarely spoke to each other, but when they did, they studied each other's throats. The youngest grabbed a pitchfork for protection long before she learned to walk and when she did learn to walk she didn't put the pitchfork down. Pa found the pig in a stall at market breathing heavily behind a sheet of corrugated tin. He felt something welling up inside him—love—and spat it onto the tin where it glistened like a chrysalis. That didn't get rid of the feeling so he brought the pig home. Ma gave Dinna' Pig his name so that no-one would forget where that pig was headed. She liked to call a spade a spade, hence her children: Mistake, Mistake 2 and Goddammit. Dinna' Pig wasn't particularly lovable; he didn't run to the side of his pen oinking sweetly when he saw a family member. He wasn't clean or smart. He sat in his shit and liked it. Goddammit thought she'd once seen him nose his own reflection in her shiny rubber boot, but she couldn't be sure. In any other farmyard, love would have slid off Dinna' Pig's oily hair, seeped from his watery eyes, bounced off the coil of his tail and landed on something fluffier. But the Family couldn't help itself—their love was stirred into the gray slop he was fed daily. It got in under his trotters, shone in the handle of the shovel they used to shovel his shit. Late one night Mistake rammed some love up Dinna' Pig's puckered little asshole. Goddammit, who'd been clutching her pitchfork in sleep, suddenly hurled it across the room. She was having a beautiful dream. It was Sunday dinner and she was the only one at the table cramming handfuls of love into her enormous mouth.

WAITRESSING IN THE ROOM WITH A THOUSAND MOONS

is difficult at best. The moons desperately want to circle something, so when a dish comes out, they dive-bomb it, bump into each other and a dusting of moon-rock falls into the food. They know the plate won't be a planet. We've been here for centuries and not once has a planet come in. I guess they do it just-in-case. Having lived most of their lives too close to everything, their sense of perspective is poor. A plate of dumplings can start to look like a solar system. Lately the moons seem to be losing hope. They're just going through the motions and their waning is way more convincing than their waxing. They no longer swarm around each swirl of steam. A red smear signals *ketchup*, not *Mars*. The food is not very good, but people keep coming. Some come with nets to sieve the sky for the tiniest butterfly-sized moons. Security is good, though—no moon has ever been smuggled out. And most of the diners look up the whole time, which makes it easy to get their attention when we recite the specials. We, the waitstaff, are waiting for the day when we come into the restaurant and find the moons circling another moon. Below them, we endlessly orbit the tables. Our leader has left us too.

WE SAT IN THEM, WE SIT IN THEM STILL

The park circles didn't fall to the ground with tiny thuds in the night like cherries. They didn't click on like girlscouts' flashlights at the sound of a coyote. They didn't work their way up through the ground like nails in an old wood floor or those mechanical platforms sequined singers climb onto below stage and then rise up on into the spotlights. We didn't think they had been there all along, like foxholes, just waiting for us to put a foot through. We tried to think of them as we did manholes—necessary interruptions in the tarmac—but they invited inspection. One park circle had a bench in it. Another was home to an aggressively friendly squirrel. Another was just a circle of grass with a sign, DO NOT WALK ON GRASS. The flowers in another did not resemble a clump of microphones. We didn't stop to consider where they came from—whether there was a park in some other dimension defined by its absences like a sheet of dough after you've cut out as many cookies as you can. When the first two appeared it *might* have been like that moment when Adam first opened his eyes, but this was before similes, before metaphors. First he would have to name every last thing in that garden, and then, only then, could he point to one thing—orchid—then another—hummingbird—and the silver threads of likeness would start to pull everything closer together. We liked the park circles because they resisted comparison. They were the one place we could be alone.

DO YOU UNDERSTAND?

No gray
rainbow
over the
blackened
land.

TERROR OF THE FUTURE / 1

If you had a talent for tealeaves,
we put you in a tent and charged
admission. Outside, people with syringes
in their arms swayed sleepily in the summer wind.
The shoe trees at home would preserve
our foot-shapes. Dried skim milk had an excellent
shelflife and the safe was rustproof, so we
scattered—made the rounds of hotels,
ordered room service and tried not to recollect
our children's quizzical looks as we showed them
the jar of quarters then locked the front door.
The polls showed no one wanted to proceed
alphabetically anymore. We were pioneers,
and we thought we might make our way back
to paradise if we spoke in the past perfect
tense. Quick as a nod, it was October
and the nectar was gone. The myocardiograph
measured our heartache and it was more
than the manuals said we could manage.
We positioned the lightship near the lemming cliff
and waited. I put on my kickpleat skirt
(best for jumping) and walked along the isthmus
looking at the icy waves. Others decided
it was high time to hike the Himalayas.
For the first time, there was goodwill
in the goldfields, across the globe.
Then the last gasps in the garage.

TERROR OF THE FUTURE / 2

A stickpin stirred in our stomachs.
When there was standing room only
we tended to get out our soapboxes.
Was it small-minded of us to want to siphon
off some sidelight from the castle?
The regime's shaved heads felt like sateen
and their salutes shot through us like good rum.
There was something remorseless about
cordoning off the red carpet with red tape.
Were they red for the wrong reason?
Not in a quadrillion years had we imagined
anyone would want proof of our prowess.
It was premodern, like the pulley.
We had portals to the future in the poolhall.
We had nuclei printed on our notepaper.
And still the night effect produced murmurs
amongst the National Guard. They didn't like
mousing about while meltwater slid like mineral oil
down the mountains. The magic lantern lurched.
We'd extracted "kingdom come" from something longer
while the original incubated in our hearts.
Even after hours of swinging back and forth
on the horizontal bars, our history stayed hooded.
We were just a gumdrop on the grid.

Our first protests were tentative:
we tapped on their taillights with teaspoons,
cut down all the swings the night before
the Festival of the Children. We didn't know
how far their patience would stretch and
we needed our applications to stay in the stack
on the spokeswoman's desk. O to be
a Somebody. O to have a hearth and not
a smudge pot. To their faces we called them
Sir and Ma'am without a trace of shame.
One Saturday they had a pig roast. Through
the binoculars, the pig looked positively Rococo
with its curls of singed flesh, its glazed snout.
We stood on the ridge and sniffed—hundreds
of us—and I thought perhaps their faces reddened
but it might have been the firelight. Proclamations
about *poultry in every household's pot* were as far
in the past as peacetime. The invalids held one-
legged races to which we wore outlandish hats
and dresses out of old organdy. We didn't have any medals
for our muddy mortals but a gang of girls rewarded
the winners with blowjobs in the alleyway behind
the mall despite the magistrate's admonitions.
Near the lending library, I found a key under a gumtree.
I carried it around with me. Someone's home was a goner.

You had to win the sweepstakes
to get a survival kit. Some of the smarter
Sunday painters kept suet and Saran Wrap
stowed amongst their stencils. My sponsor
disappeared with nary a splash. I didn't speculate.
I said he was "snowed under." All we ever did
together was play "Simon Says" and try to outrun
our shadows. It was a rotten routine and I'm not
going to romanticize it. I wouldn't have put ribbons
on his wreath but I was hoping to qualify for
the preharvest and a few jars of preserves.
In the meantime I sent my remaining relatives
postcards with phoenixes on the front.
No need to be a pessimist and think about
the family plot. Yes, the panic-stricken and pain-ridden
continued to dive into the Pacific, but one
could get overstimulated thinking about it.
I was no onlooker. I went shopping for
a new look. I studied myths. I even invented
a motto for myself: Never Say Mayday
While There's Still Marzipan. When I was feeling
low-spirited, it helped to think of the lion
who was being given only lichen to eat.
The lily-livered wouldn't look through the lens.
I looked and saw that the scientists
in the laboratory were looking for keywords
in the Judgment Book, still hadn't jettisoned
that piece of junk. It was time to make a home
in the hedge and try not to hear the gunshots.
So what if the grass was really green glass?

Technically, "lonely me" was a tautology.
No one had ever stuffed carnations
in my tailpipe or planted a symbolic
lipsticked kiss on the swingdoor
to my kitchen. When you appeared,
I knew I was in a race against the sun
before they took you away on a stretcher.
I spruced up the counters with spit
and a sponge—I wiped my slot machine
mouth clean. I shut the door, locked it.
I shouldn't have—you were just here
to shop—but I was way past worrying
about the seven deadly sins. In the show
about the sea lion and natural selection,
he got scratches from his lover too. Even
in rope restraints, you were a scorcher, sweetie.
The radio said we needed to repeople.
I should have given you a running start;
I gave you roses. I persevered—I professed
the principles of capillary attraction,
made you a plaster-of-Paris statue of a peacock,
wrote hundreds of haiku. The odds on you
loving me were a thousand to one, but there you were:
nibbling my toes in your nightshirt,
kissing me on the mouth in the mudroom.
My chest felt like it had undergone mitosis,
it ached so. I marveled at the maple syrup moon—
it had a luster unlike any linoleum.
We watched the lake breeze lift the leaves
through the keyhole. Inventory was low
and we were out of holy oil. Helicopters
landed on the hospital roof
every hour then every half hour.

The swallows formed subtitles for the clouds.
Sometimes you read them out loud to me:
The superexaminer will smell like sulfur,
a statement no less ominous than the stone lily
we stumbled across in the garden, stricken
there by some aggressive stare. When you wore
stilettos (you always wore stilettos), steady-going
was out of the question. As stammer is to
statement so was your wobbling to walking.
Like everything else, the sponging house
by the shore was swathed in smaze and hard
to find, but once there you could watch
through the window as sailors soaped off
their shipworms and schemed about getting back
out to sea. I thought that might be an idea
for you and me, but you, who hated a parade
and loved a recession, wanted to watch the tide go out
without us. One morning, I found you crying over
the blender—you'd read "pulse" as "repulse."
After that, you started hiding pennies in the playhouse
sheltered by the parentheses of spruce trees,
as if *that* constituted a plan. I followed all your directions—
to the North River where there were no fish, then back
to the near-point, where opthamologically speaking
you could best keep an eye on me.

TERROR OF THE FUTURE / 7

We both suffered from telesthesia,
how we disconnected our circuit boards
differed. Me: tall drinks in tankards. You:
endless rereadings of *The Sun Also Rises*.
The stretcher-bearers headed south—
who knows why—but they skedaddled,
and the sudden silence in the sidestreets
was like a shade pulled down over a view
we hadn't liked to begin with. I tuned my scanner
to the rumor-mill. Someone resigned.
It barely registered: everyone rose in rank
accordingly, like the reflex that lives in your knee.
Rangers kept pruning the trees, on principle,
pretending our predicament was temporary.
I collected plastic, melted it down, made myself
a nightstick, never mind that even my embryonic
mid-brain knew no one would come near me
but you. When the mail came, we still ran like mad
to get it. We read job descriptions outloud
to one another, *king, keyman,* until our jaws ached,
then added the circulars to the fire and watched
the ashes float off over the lake. I wrote your
initials everywhere (on each step of the stairs)
until you informed me you'd changed
your name and got out your India rubber.
When had you gone incognito on me?

Your breath was sweet like swamp azaleas.
You weren't going to survive this—none of us
were—but who signed me up to stroke your hand
while the stratocumulus gathered sullenly in the sky?
S.O.S., I repeated quietly as I made you a soft-boiled egg
then carried it upstairs in slow-motion along with a glass
with the last of the sherry. *Saturday night special!*
I announced, trying to look sanguine. I had a vase
but no rose. That night, there was no one
at the rendezvous point, I checked. I'd been reluctant
to go myself. The sunset was like a protractor laid
on the horizon line and the powder that fell
from the planes made point lace of the tarmac.
We were at that part of the plot line where
the planchette swiftly spells out PHAETHON
on the ouija board. Not what I'd pick, given
the choice, though I don't believe in open sesames
into the next world anyway. In the olden days
it would have been time for that last dance number.
Instead here I was feeding you narcotics
and trimming your nails. Your horoscope read:
You have an infectious smile. Mine said:
Check the glove compartment.

TERROR OF THE FUTURE / 9

The teacups tied to strings along the walkway
stayed silent, had no warning songs to sing.
We shook talc onto our tastebuds
and watched the skyrockets, starry-eyed,
until night blacked them out like a giant
malevolent Sharpie. Scouts gathered
in the square and surveyed the Room
For Rent signs. In this and only this did we have
supply and no demand. It was a long time
since anyone had felt a quiver on the railroad.
We argued timetables, regardless,
(I was just glad you were speaking to me).
You wanted to go to the provinces.
I wanted to see the palace. Of course,
given the state of the ozone, we weren't
going anywhere. We weren't outdoorsy
anyway. Our anoraks were moth-eaten
for a reason. You said, *I am morose, a new kind*
of rose. I pointed hopefully at my foot and said
mistletoe? No. You wouldn't get within a meter
of me. Later, when your lungs filled with liquid,
you might have said *love*, you might have said *leave*.
I said *I love you too* and left the room.
There was no ice storm, no helicoptered-in help,
no Hollywood ending. Just a gasp and then
no more you, which meant the end of me too.

TERROR OF THE FUTURE / 10

Sweetheart, there's no one on the street.
I attached the speakers to the steeple
but even on its loudest setting, the stereo
gets no reaction. If you ask me, (ask me,
please) the split screen of the brain
needs a sounding board, doesn't like the only
signals in the skyway to be its own synapses,
doesn't want to go solo in the sandbox.
You're. Not. Breathing. Let's see: memories.
I remember the rocking chair that was always
in the repair shop for liking to rock backward
but not forward. I remember the price
of a pressurized suit. I remember the red ribbon
in your hair. I remember when pandemonium
was possible. O there's no way to nectarize this moment—
it's entirely without sweetness. In just a minute
it'll be match point and of course the world wins.
It's not a matter of life and death, it's life or
death. Here in the grove, after jar after jar
of grain alcohol, the sun looks like a halo,
then a noose. Give me a helping hand,
historian. Help me with that "or."

THE INVENTION OF LOVE

The cave woman and cave man lie side by side, each head filled with bright images the other can't see. Even when they press their ears or mouths or noses together, the skull wall is still in the way. In one head there is a gazelle staining a pool with its bleeding hoof. In the other, a patchwork of faces and forest fastened together with thorns. They look at each other. Is that a world in the other's brimming eye? No, just the cave reflected, cold and dark and home. They bump globes sadly. The gazelle is fading. The forest is just the forest outside. "I am hungry," one gestures. "I am hungry too," gestures the other.

THE INVENTION OF FILM

The cave woman throws her berries into the fire. She is tired of berries. They taste not-sweet, not-good. She glowers at the flames. In the fire the berries are beginning to wrinkle. One has a chin, another a grimace like Man in Cave by Stream. One branch of berries starts to glow and the berries begin to swell. One explodes with a loud pop. The cave woman screams and scurries away. Another berry pops. Then another. The cave man peers into the fire. The cave woman creeps back and watches with him until all the berries have popped. She throws another branch on the fire. Take Two. Action.

YOU HAVE MY EYES

Give them back.

TEMPORARY FAMILY

Sister tries out her tantrum. It requires a hamster and ends with a trill and five fading sobs. Auntie teeters towards the mantelpiece. Dad is on the faux-phone with a friend. No one's speaking to him because last time he kept cornering the client for unscripted fatherly chats. Mom snips at a streamer with her pinking shears. Maybe *this* time it'll be a birthday. When the buzzer finally goes off, it's one last shot for Auntie. They grab the props from the basket by the door—the sweater knitted just far enough that it could be for anybody of any size, a broken china dog to blame on Brother. They leave Monopoly behind because someone's stolen all the little green houses, leaving only the red hotels. In the van, they read the girl's file, memorize their personalities. Grandma's trying dementia this time around so there's nothing new she needs to know. The front door opens. The family swarms the orphan.

I WOULD HAVE STAYED

The vinedresser
of the Belvedere
having found
a very strange
lizard,
Leonardo
made some wings
of the scales
of other
lizards and fastened
them on its back
with a mixture
of quicksilver,
so that
they trembled
when it walked;
and having made
for it eyes, horns,
and a beard,
he tamed it
and kept it
in a box,
but all his friends
to whom he showed it
used to run away
from fear.

NEW FRIENDS

Plant me
just below
the potatoes.
I won't complain
if their root patterns
don't exactly
match my synapses—
chances are they'll be
closer than lightning
or anything else
I've found
aboveground.

ODE TO THE DOUBLE-NATURED SIDES OF THINGS

God and the angels arrive in Eden to find only a scattering of stems on the ground. Noticing how the angels' wings fall from left to right as they bend over the stems, God invents a more flexible forgiveness. Things change just slightly. The usual botany class—two rows of long tables, students on either side with wildflowers in vases between them—keeps its format, but now, if a boy puts down his reference book and stares instead at a dot of green on the cheek of the girl across from him, his essay "How a Leaf So Tiny Got on Her Cheek" is relevant, may even warrant an "A." Above the sky may be dark. Below the corn may be dry. Some days recess has to be on the west side of school because it's raining on the east side.

STRAWBERRY ON THE DRAWBRIDGE

I tried eating one there on the bridge's faultline, listening out for the dispatcher's radio so that I'd know if a ship was coming and the road was about to split in two—I love when roads give up on going anywhere and point up toward the heavens. But standing on tiptoe on that crenellated bit of metal (tongue in groove, groove in tongue) didn't give me the right feeling. Ships were few. And it made me imagine *myself* being split in two, like St. Simon, martyred lengthwise down the middle, which was a feeling I already knew.

For my experiment, I needed an abandoned drawbridge. I found it in Delaware. It was no star, with its rusted rivets and peeling paint, but it was what I was looking for. I got out my orange cones and policetape and cordoned off the area. As a last touch, I put on a uniform I'd bought at the Salvation Army. Then I made a little mound of earth right in the center of the bridge and planted my strawberry plant. I put a bell jar over it and sat next to it, shifting every half hour so that my shadow wouldn't block the sun. Sometimes, I sat in the control box and polished the controls. Finally, one day the plant sprouted a tiny green strawberry dead center and a week later it was good and red and round. On that long-anticipated day, I pressed play on the tape recorder: *Clowns to the left of me, jokers to the right— here I am, stuck in the middle with you.* On the word "middle," I lowered the lever and raised my binoculars to my eyes.

The bridge groaned and began to open. Some of the roots went to the left, some to the right. The bell jar wobbled, then toppled into the water with a celebratory splash. Soil sifted into the river. And the strawberry hung there, suspended between its two sets of roots and stems like an atom in a science experiment. First the skin, with its little grainy seeds strained, then split. Then as the fleshy part broke open, I could see the pale V of its interior and when that split too, the words finally separated into straw and berry and draw and bridge, and like recombinant DNA, formed new ones. Strawbridge. Drawberry. In the world they conjured the straw bridges were sharp and shiny, too delicate to cross, and there in the berry patches were the artists, islanded at their easels.

SETTING THE TABLE

To cut through night you'll need your sharpest scissors. Cut around the birch, the bump of the bird nest on its lowest limb. Then with your nail scissors, trim around the baby beaks waiting for worms to fall from the sky. Snip around the lip of the mailbox and the pervert's shoe peeking out from behind the Chevy. Before dawn, rip the silhouette from the sky and drag it inside. Frame the long black stripe and hang it in the dining room. Sleep. When you wake, redo the scene as day in doily. Now you have a lacy fence, a huge cherry blossom of a holly bush, a birch sugared with snow. Frame the white version and hang it opposite the black. Get your dinner and eat it between the two scenes. Your food will taste just right.

NOTES

The poems "The Future of Terror" and "Terror of the Future" were inspired by making lists of the words in the dictionary between "future" and "terror." They are not strict abecedarian poems because they are not acrostics, but they do mimic the abecedarius's alphabetical footsteps. The words "future" and "terror" act like "A" and "B"—they were the markers that mattered. For a longer essay on this subject published by *American Poet*, please visit www.mattheaharvey.info.

The text of the poem "I Would Have Stayed" is a lineated version of a quote from Giorgio Vasari's *Lives of the Most Eminent Painters, Sculptors, and Architects*. Only the title is mine.

© R. CASPER

MATTHEA HARVEY is the author of two previous books of poetry, *Pity the Bathtub Its Forced Embrace of the Human Form* and *Sad Little Breathing Machine*, and a children's book, *The Little General and the Giant Snowflake*, illustrated by Elizabeth Zechel. She teaches poetry at Sarah Lawrence College and is a contributing editor to *jubilat* and *BOMB*. She lives in Brooklyn.

The text of *Modern Life* is set in Adobe Jenson Pro, a typeface drawn by Robert Slimbach and based on late-fifteenth-century types by the printer Nicolas Jenson. Book design by Ann Sudmeier. Composition by Prism Publishing Center. Manufactured by Versa Press on acid-free paper.